YOUR PASSPORT TO
EGYPT

>> by Golriz Golkar >>

CONTENT CONSULTANT

Rita Lucarelli, PhD
Egyptologist
University of California, Berkeley

CAPSTONE PRESS
a capstone imprint

Published by Capstone Press, an imprint of Capstone
1710 Roe Crest Drive, North Mankato, Minnesota 56003
capstonepub.com

Library of Congress Cataloging-in-Publication Data is available on the Library of Congress website
ISBN: 9781663959263 (hardcover)
ISBN: 9781666321845 (paperback)
ISBN: 9781666321852 (ebook PDF)

Summary: Explore the sights, traditions, and daily lives of the people of Egypt! Learn about the customs, traditions, food, celebrations, and landmarks that distinguish Egypt from other countries.

Editorial Credits
Editor: Marie Pearson; Designer: Colleen McLaren; Production Specialist: Christine Ha and Laura Manthe

Image Credits
Newscom: Ahmed Gomaa/Xinhua News Agency, 23, Amr Sayed/ZUMA Press, 25; Red Line Editorial, 5; Shutterstock: agsaz, 14, AlexAnton, Cover, Amr Hassanein, 29, Daily Travel Photos, 9, Filip Bjorkman, (vector) Cover, Flipser, (passport) design element, javarman, 7, Loveshop, Cover, Merydolla, 13, MicroOne, (visa stamps) design element, mohsen nabil, 27, Nacho Such, 19, Novie Charleen Magne, 24, Oleksandr Kalinichenko, 10, pingebat, (stamps) design element, waupee08, 17, Yevhenii Dubinko, (stamps) design element

CONTENTS

CHAPTER ONE
WELCOME TO EGYPT!.............................. 4

CHAPTER TWO
HISTORY OF EGYPT 8

CHAPTER THREE
EXPLORE EGYPT 12

CHAPTER FOUR
DAILY LIFE 18

CHAPTER FIVE
HOLIDAYS AND CELEBRATIONS 22

CHAPTER SIX
SPORTS AND RECREATION............................ 26

GLOSSARY 30
READ MORE/INTERNET SITES........................... 31
INDEX 32

Words in **bold** are in the glossary.

WELCOME TO EGYPT!

The hot desert sun is setting. Three giant pyramids rise into the golden sky. They were the tombs of ancient Egyptian kings. Nearby, a giant statue rises from the sands. It is part lion and part human. Like the pyramids, it was built long ago. These are the pyramids and Great Sphinx of Giza in Egypt. They are the remains of one of the world's most ancient civilizations.

Egypt is a country in northeastern Africa. It connects Africa and Asia. The country is mostly desert. There are also wetlands, oases, and river islands.

FACT

In the 200s **BCE**, a mathematician named Philo or Philon made a list of amazing structures. The list is now known as the Seven Wonders of the Ancient World. The Great Pyramid of Giza is the only one standing today.

MAP OF EGYPT

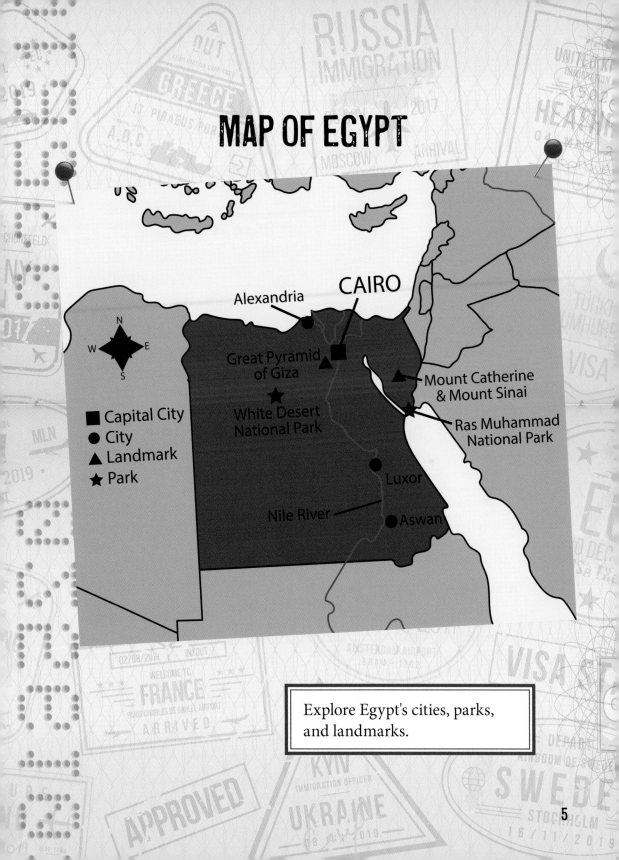

Alexandria

CAIRO

Great Pyramid
of Giza

Mount Catherine
& Mount Sinai

White Desert
National Park

Ras Muhammad
National Park

■ Capital City
● City
▲ Landmark
★ Park

Luxor

Nile River

Aswan

Explore Egypt's cities, parks,
and landmarks.

FACT FILE

OFFICIAL NAME: .... ARAB REPUBLIC OF EGYPT
POPULATION: 106,437,241
LAND AREA: .... 384,345 SQ. MI. (995,450 SQ KM)
CAPITAL: .... CAIRO
MONEY: .... EGYPTIAN POUND
GOVERNMENT: .... PRESIDENTIAL REPUBLIC
LANGUAGE: .... ARABIC
GEOGRAPHY: Egypt is located in northeastern Africa. It is where the African and Asian continents meet. It borders the Mediterranean Sea to the north. Sudan lies to the south. Libya is to the west, and Israel and the Red Sea are to the east.
NATURAL RESOURCES: Egypt has petroleum, gas, iron, phosphates, and limestone.

Visitors can discover ancient temples. They can visit museums and outdoor markets. Some may ride boats on the Nile River. Others may ride camels across the desert sands.

EGYPTIAN PEOPLE

More than 100 million people live in Egypt. About half of all Egyptians live in cities. The other half live in the countryside. Most Egyptians are Muslim.

Alexandria is one of the largest cities in Egypt.

Egypt is also home to several **native** peoples. Nubian people live in southern Egypt. Amazigh people live in the west. Bedouin people are **nomads**. They live on the Sinai Peninsula in the northeast.

Arabic is Egypt's official language. Native peoples often speak their own languages too. Egyptians are proud of their rich **culture**. Museums around the world hold Egyptian art and artifacts. Egyptians also produce popular music, literature, and films.

CHAPTER TWO

HISTORY OF EGYPT

The first Egyptian **dynasty** ruled around 3000 BCE. Pharaohs ruled Egypt for the next 2,000 years. Pharaohs built many of the monuments still standing today. Egyptians traded goods throughout Africa and Asia. They traded items such as gold, grain, and a writing surface called papyrus. In exchange, they got wood and other building materials.

FACT

The ancient Egyptians invented many things used today. These inventions include paper, ink, makeup, toothbrushes, and toothpaste.

CHANGING RULERS

In about 1000 BCE, pharaohs began to lose power. Egypt split into smaller regions. Different families ruled these regions. In 332 BCE, Alexander the Great of Greece took control. He died in 323 BCE. Ptolemy I became the new ruler. His dynasty lasted until 30 BCE.

The Pyramids of Giza were built from the 2500s to the 2400s BCE.

For the next 700 years, Romans and Byzantines ruled Egypt. Christianity was the main religion at this time. In 642 **CE**, Arab Muslims took control. They ruled for hundreds of years. In the 1500s, Ottoman Turks took control. They also ruled for hundreds of years.

The Suez Canal remains an important shipping route for transporting goods.

MODERN EGYPT

The United Kingdom **occupied** Egypt in 1882. The UK government wanted to control the Suez Canal. The canal was the shortest sailing route from Asia to Europe. This made it cheaper to ship goods. In 1952, Egypt gained **independence** from the United Kingdom. Egypt became a presidential **republic**.

In the 1970s, Egypt fought several wars with Israel. A peace agreement was signed in 1979. In 2011, there was a large protest about the government. Longtime president Hosni Mubarak was overthrown.

TIMELINE OF EGYPTIAN HISTORY

ABOUT 3000 BCE: The first Egyptian dynasty begins.

332 BCE: Alexander the Great conquers Egypt.

642 CE: Arab Muslims conquer Egypt.

969: Cairo becomes the Egyptian capital.

1517: Egypt falls under the Ottoman Empire's rule.

1798: Napoleon Bonaparte's army tries to invade Egypt but fails.

1869: The Suez Canal is completed.

1882: The United Kingdom occupies Egypt.

1922: Fuad I becomes king while British forces continue to occupy Egypt.

1953: Muhammad Najib becomes president. Egypt becomes a republic despite unfair presidential elections.

1973: Egypt and Syria fight with Israel over lost land. Egypt regains the Sinai Peninsula.

2011: The Arab Spring uprising overthrows President Hosni Mubarak.

2014: The new constitution bans political parties based on religion.

Since then, Egypt has officially had democratic elections. However, candidates running against the president usually drop out of the race. This means the president stays in office.

CHAPTER THREE

EXPLORE EGYPT

Egypt is full of places to explore. Cairo is the capital of Egypt. It is the country's largest city. The Khan El-Khalili is the most popular market. Vendors there sell souvenirs, jewelry, and more. The Egyptian Museum houses Egyptian artifacts. Many were found in pharaohs' tombs.

Visitors can see the Citadel. This is a massive fortress built starting in 1176 CE. It has a **mosque** and several museums. It was home to Egypt's rulers for hundreds of years. Visitors also go to the top of the Cairo Tower. They get a bird's-eye view of the city.

EXCITING CITIES

Luxor is home to the Valley of the Kings. Pharaohs were buried there. One famous tomb belongs to King Tutankhamun. It was found full of treasure.

Small shops sell a variety of items at the Khan El-Khalili market.

Statues of Ramses II line the entrance of the Luxor Temple.

Visitors can see the Luxor and Karnak Temples. People worshipped gods and goddesses at the temples. The columns are decorated with **hieroglyphs**. Luxor is also a popular spot for boat rides. Visitors sail down the Nile in wooden sailboats called feluccas.

Alexandria is the second-largest city in Egypt. It has sandy beaches and outdoor markets. There are museums and ruins dating from the 200s BCE to the 600s CE. This was when Greeks and Romans ruled Egypt.

Aswan is a quiet city in the Nile River Valley. Visitors can see the Philae Temple. This temple was first built around 280 BCE. People worshipped the goddess Isis there. Visitors can enjoy local Nubian food. Aswan has granite **quarries**. Many of Egypt's monuments were made with stone found there.

NATURAL AREAS

Egypt's landscape is a mix of desert and fertile land. Northern Egypt has fertile valleys near the Nile River. They are surrounded by desert. The Nile runs north through Egypt. It drains into the Mediterranean Sea. It is the longest river in the world.

THE NILE RIVER

The Nile River is an important source of water in the desert. Springtime rains in the Ethiopian highlands make the river rise. The river floods. The water adds nutrients to the soil. This makes the soil good for growing crops. The ancient Egyptians built canals to water crops. Today, the Nile River remains important for Egyptians.

Southern Egypt is mostly desert and low mountains. Mount Catherine is on the Sinai Peninsula. It is the tallest mountain in Egypt. Nearby, Mount Sinai is a holy place. Jews, Christians, and Muslims travel there.

ANIMAL PARADISE

Egypt has many national parks. They are home to **endangered** plants and animals. Visitors can go bird-watching at Lake Qarun. This lake is a protected area. Many of the country's bird species live there. Ras Muhammad National Park is on the Red Sea. The park has coral reefs. The reefs are perfect for snorkeling. Visitors can see the colorful fish there. More than 100 kinds of fish also swim in the Nile River.

WHITE DESERT NATIONAL PARK

White Desert National Park has white rock formations. Minerals such as calcium make the rocks white. Sandstorms shaped the rocks. Some look like animals. Visitors can enjoy a meal at a Bedouin restaurant. Some visitors camp overnight.

The Nile River provides water for plants and animals.

CHAPTER FOUR

DAILY LIFE

About half of Egyptians live in cities. Many live in apartments. They wear Western-style clothes such as jeans, T-shirts, and dresses. They shop for food at supermarkets.

The other half live in the countryside. Some live in stone or mud houses near the Nile River. Both men and women often wear traditional clothes. These simple outfits have layers of light fabric that cover the arms and legs. Some villagers are farmers. They grow grains, fruits, and cotton. Other villagers work in offices or shops. A village usually has a mosque or church.

Egyptian children must attend school from age 6 to 17. Students who pass a national exam may then study at either a trade school or secondary school. The best secondary students may then attend a university.

Some people in Egypt choose to wear traditional clothes, while others wear Western clothes.

RELIGION

Nearly 90 percent of Egyptians are Muslim. Many pray five times a day. Muslims worship at mosques on Fridays. About 10 percent of Egyptians are Christians. They attend church on Sundays.

FOOD AND DRINK

Egyptians eat many tasty dishes. The national dish is a stew called ful medames. It has fava beans, vegetables, and spices. It is eaten with flatbread. Coffee and tea are popular drinks. Desserts include pastries and puddings. Honey, figs, or dates sweeten the puddings.

People often buy food from street carts. Taameya are Egyptian falafels. They are made with fried fava beans. Koshary is a pasta, rice, and lentil dish. It is served with tomato sauce. Beef and lamb are common meats. Shawarma are meat sandwiches served on flatbread. Hawawshi is a minced-meat sandwich served in pita bread. Kofta kebabs are meat skewers.

BASBOUSA

Basbousa is a popular coconut cake. Many Egyptian bakeries sell it.

Cake Ingredients:
- 2 cups semolina
- 1 cup shredded coconut
- ⅓ cup sugar
- 1 teaspoon baking soda
- ½ cup melted butter
- 1 cup plain yogurt
- ⅓ cup whole roasted almonds

Syrup Ingredients:
- 2 cups sugar
- 1 ½ cups water
- 1 teaspoon lemon juice

Basbousa Directions:

1. Preheat the oven to 400°F. Grease a pie dish with butter. Set it aside.
2. In a large bowl, mix the semolina, coconut, sugar, baking soda, and butter. Mix the ingredients with your hands. Add the yogurt. Mix until the blend is thick.
3. Press the mixture into the pie dish. Use a knife to cut lines in the mixture, creating diamond-shaped portions. Place an almond inside each diamond.
4. Bake the cake for 30 minutes or until it's a dark golden brown.
5. While the cake is baking, mix the syrup ingredients in a saucepan. Boil the mixture for 10 minutes. Set aside.
6. When the cake is done, cut it along the diamond shapes again. Pour the cooled syrup over the hot cake. Let it sit for 10 minutes and then serve.

HOLIDAYS AND CELEBRATIONS

Egyptians of all religions celebrate Sham El-Nessim. It marks the arrival of spring. It has been celebrated since ancient times. Egyptians boil and decorate eggs. The eggs are eaten with meats and a fish dish called feseekh.

NATIONAL HOLIDAYS

Egyptians celebrate Revolution Day on July 23. The country won its independence from the United Kingdom on this day in 1952. Armed Forces Day is on October 6. It honors the day the Sinai Peninsula was won back from Israel. Both holidays have military parades and fireworks.

FACT

During Sham El-Nessim, Egyptians write wishes on decorated eggs and hang them from trees.

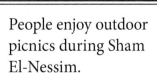

People enjoy outdoor picnics during Sham El-Nessim.

Muslim Egyptians eat a meal after sunset during Ramadan.

RELIGIOUS HOLIDAYS

Muslim Egyptians celebrate Ramadan. For one month, people do not eat from sunrise until sunset. They visit friends and family. They attend a mosque. At the end of Ramadan, Muslims celebrate Eid al-Fitr. They feast on traditional dishes and nut cookies called kahk. Children receive gifts and new clothes.

Many Coptic Christians attend a Christmas Eve service.

Coptic Christians follow an old form of calendar for their holidays. They celebrate Christmas on January 7. They do not eat animal products for 43 days before Christmas Eve. Then they enjoy meat dishes. Children receive presents on Christmas Day.

CHAPTER SIX

SPORTS AND RECREATION

Soccer is Egypt's national sport. Most Egyptians follow the top two rival teams, Al Ahly and Zamalek. These popular teams have won many national and continental championships. The Pharaohs are the national team. They have won the African Cup of Nations several times.

OTHER SPORTS AND ACTIVITIES

Egyptians also enjoy volleyball and basketball. They watch weightlifting and wrestling matches. Judo, swimming, and tennis are popular sports to play. Children enjoy playing soccer, tennis, and squash.

Mohamed Salah (left) is one of the most famous soccer players from Egypt.

SEEGA

Seega is an Egyptian board game. It takes two players. Using a ruler, draw a game board of five squares by five squares on a piece of paper. There will be a total of 25 small squares. Draw an X in the middle square. Each player should cut 12 small squares of paper for their playing pieces. Both players should color all their pieces in a different color from the other player's pieces.

1. Players take turns placing two pieces each anywhere on the board, except on the X square. Player Two is the person who places pieces on the board second.

2. When all pieces are on the board, Player Two begins by moving one piece. A piece can move by one square either horizontally or vertically. Diagonal moves are not allowed. The X square may now be used.

3. The goal is to capture an enemy piece. To do this, a player must trap an enemy piece between two of his or her own pieces either horizontally or vertically. The captured enemy piece is removed from the board. Pieces on the X square cannot be captured. But they can be used to capture an enemy's piece.

4. If a player captures an enemy piece, the player can move the same piece again. If no capture is made, the other player goes.

5. The player who captures all of the enemy's pieces first wins.

Dance is an important part of Egyptian culture. Belly dancing is performed by women at weddings and other events.

Some people enjoy hiking in Egypt's deserts.

Men in southern Egypt perform tahtib. This is an ancient martial art that uses sticks. Today, it is performed as a dance.

Egyptians also enjoy their country's natural beauty. They hike in the mountains. They ride boats on the Nile. Egypt offers tasty foods and ancient ruins. There are many fun ways to pass the time.

GLOSSARY

BCE/CE
BCE means Before Common Era, or before year one. CE means Common Era, or the years starting with year one

culture (KUHL-chur)
the customs and way of life for a group of people

dynasty (DYE-nuh-stee)
a series of rulers from the same family

endangered (en-DAYN-jurd)
in danger of becoming extinct

hieroglyph (HIGH-ruh-glif)
a picture used in a system of writing

independence (in-di-PEN-duhns)
the freedom a country has to govern itself

mosque (MOSK)
a building where Muslims gather together to worship

native (NAY-tuhv)
a person who was born in a particular country or place; also, something tied to a certain location

nomad (NOH-mad)
someone who often moves from one place to another

occupy (AHK-yoo-pie)
to take control of a country and station soldiers there

quarry (KWOR-ee)
an open pit where stones are dug up for building

republic (ri-PUB-lik)
a type of government where people elect their political leaders and president

READ MORE

Cleveland-Peck, Patricia. *The Secrets of Tutankhamun: Egypt's Boy King and His Incredible Tomb.* New York: Bloomsbury, 2018.

Flynn, Sarah Wassner. *Ancient Egypt.* Washington, D.C.: National Geographic, 2019.

Honovich, Nancy. *1,000 Facts About Ancient Egypt.* Washington, D.C.: National Geographic, 2019.

INTERNET SITES

DK Find Out!: Ancient Egypt
dkfindout.com/us/history/ancient-egypt/

National Geographic Kids: Egypt
kids.nationalgeographic.com/geography/countries/article /egypt

Wonderopolis: Who Built Egypt's Great Pyramids?
wonderopolis.org/wonder/Who-Built-Egypt%E2%80%99s -Great-Pyramids

INDEX

Alexandria, 14

Aswan, 15

Cairo, 6, 11, 12

dance, 28–29

food, 15, 18, 20, 21, 22, 29

Lake Qarun, 16

Luxor, 12, 14

Mubarak, Hosni, 10, 11

Nile River, 6, 14–16, 18, 29

pyramids, 4

Ras Muhammad National Park, 16

religion, 6, 9, 11, 16, 20, 24–25

Revolution Day, 22

Sham El-Nessim, 22

sports, 26

ABOUT THE AUTHOR

Golriz Golkar is the author of more than 40 nonfiction books for children. Inspired by her work as an elementary school teacher, she loves to write the kinds of books that students are excited to read. Golriz holds a B.A. in American literature and culture from UCLA and an Ed.M. in language and literacy from the Harvard Graduate School of Education. She loves to travel and study languages. Golriz lives in France with her husband and young daughter, Ariane. She thinks children are the very best teachers, and she loves learning from her daughter every day.

OTHER BOOKS IN THIS SERIES

YOUR PASSPORT TO ARGENTINA
YOUR PASSPORT TO AUSTRALIA
YOUR PASSPORT TO CHINA
YOUR PASSPORT TO ECUADOR
YOUR PASSPORT TO EL SALVADOR
YOUR PASSPORT TO ENGLAND
YOUR PASSPORT TO ETHIOPIA
YOUR PASSPORT TO FRANCE
YOUR PASSPORT TO GUATEMALA
YOUR PASSPORT TO IRAN

YOUR PASSPORT TO ITALY
YOUR PASSPORT TO KENYA
YOUR PASSPORT TO MEXICO
YOUR PASSPORT TO PERU
YOUR PASSPORT TO RUSSIA
YOUR PASSPORT TO SOUTH KOREA
YOUR PASSPORT TO SPAIN
YOUR PASSPORT TO SRI LANKA
YOUR PASSPORT TO TURKEY